Praise for N

I am in humble awe of how Kerani Marie wields the artistry of words and imagery to carve out a sacred permission—a space where we can feel the raw, unguarded impact of being a fully sensing, fully realized human being. Her generosity in revealing the vast spectrum of her lived journey—from agony to ecstasy, from collapse to transcendence, from shadow to radiance—opens a pathway straight into the heart of paradox. It is a gift that touches one's very Soul.

With a kind of raw elegance, Kerani Marie offers language that sings through the bones and breath of the reader. As she allows herself to feel it all, she quietly, powerfully ushers us toward our own depths and our own heights.

A living cauldron of creativity, she reminds us that each life is a canvas, and each of us a living artist. Her poetry becomes a ceremony of remembrance—a testament that the more we are willing to feel, the more profoundly our pure being can be offered back to life itself.

Enocha "Ranjita" Ryan
Transformational Healing Artist
Sedona, AZ

Naked at the Altar of Soul touched me in ways I didn't expect—ways that reached beneath the surface and stirred something ancient within me.

Reading Kerani's words felt like looking into a mirror I didn't know I needed. Each passage permitted me—to feel everything, to honor the confusion and the clarity, to surrender to the tides of emotion rather than resisting their pull. Kerani's writing doesn't just express; it awakens. It speaks the unspoken and dignifies the journey of breaking down and becoming anew. Thank you, Kerani, for this offering. It is not just a book. It is a threshold.

In your art of storytelling, I felt the ache of truth and the grace of transformation. You've captured the sacred mess of being human—the alchemy of loss, the mystery of grief, the quiet, radiant strength it takes to live through the in-between. You reminded me that the very act of staying soft in times of upheaval is not weakness...it is ceremony. Thank you for this offering.

Milli Cannata
Real Estate Broker, Ceremonial and Retreat Facilitator
Sonoma County, CA

With great vulnerability, transparency, and courage, Kerani uncovers seemingly contradictory emotions and experiences, holding them gently up to the light so that in the sharing of her soul's journey, she gives us a map to ourselves. Suddenly, we feel less alone.

As she writes of her path of descent, dissolution, and rebirth...from order, to disorder, to reorder and back again and again, we witness her deep transformation, and we feel more willing to step into the fire of our own soul quest.

It is a gift that her poetry unflinchingly stirs the ingredients of love, loss, and healing in her fiery cauldron because the medicinal soup she serves is deeply complex, layered, and full of wisdom. Thank you, dear woman, for singing your soul's song into existence so that we who are lucky enough to read it see ourselves reflected in the mirror!

Sharon Collaros
Poet, Student of Life, and Ordinary Mystic
Ohio

These poems are a tremendous gift and transmission from Kerani Marie. Not mired in concepts, they convey living insight rooted in raw emotions and deep wisdom from grief, rage, and despair. No matter how loud the howls, deep the pain, or uncomfortable the truths, Kerani Marie is devoted to what presents itself. These poems are a journal of that steadfast devotion. And, it is a story of rebirth as she dims her ego, lets go of old patterns, and opens to extraordinary grace and love. Her poetry chronicles it all so that we feel an intimation of what is possible.

Pam Taylor
Artist, Author, and Educator
Salem, OR

NAKED AT THE ALTAR OF SOUL

Poetry from the Soul Realms of the Underworld, Mystery, and Remembering

KERANI MARIE

ISBN: 979-8-9902092-6-8

Front cover painting by Kerani Marie

Cover design by Melanie Pahlmann

SoWISE Creations
www.SoWISEcreations.com

PRINTED IN THE USA

Dedicated to the sacred quest of
listening to the soul's whispers,
as the Mystery unveils what
has long remained unseen.

Author's Introduction

I have found poetry offers me a freedom beyond rules, a space where intuition and a felt sense of emergence guides the way. Poetry fosters a profound connection with the soul—a place where I gather my raw truths, down to my bare bones, where paradoxes can meet, illuminating the wisdom of my heart.

My poems are flashpoints, moments when something long held in silence breaks open into the physical realm. Opposites collide, old truths crumble, and from the rubble of chaos and destruction a portal opens.

The life–death–rebirth cycle happens repeatedly in my poetry. Sometimes this alchemy stirs quietly, in a season of stillness or reflection, as a hibernation of the soul, until the spark of creative fire erupts like a volcano. New ideas flood in born from the raw elements, and my shifting directions of life become poems.

Poetry is my way of living within the current of transformation, it asks me to reorient, to embody a new way of being. The only certainty is that something has changed, and in this newness, listening becomes everything. It is here, in the Mystery, I am nourished, as my creative expression requires me to listen to what comes through my poetry.

The poetry I share with you was written between the autumn of 2018, and the autumn of 2025. These eight years carried me through profound loss and deep transformation. In a five-month period, my marriage ended, my father and brother passed, and I had to sell and pack up three homes— my personal home, my spiritual center, and my parents' home. I then purchased and moved into my new home in Sedona, Arizona.

On the other side of this polarity, I was led to Sedona, where the red rock canyons welcomed me to my soul's home. In Sedona, I am embraced by a vibrant community; I began painting again, I built the Underworld Womb Cave and held women's retreats and ceremonies. I have a whole section about the Womb Cave later in the book.

Some of the more recent poems were birthed during my current five-month journey with Shakti Kundalini Ma. I have been home bound 90% of the time since the shakti energy has been surging in my body. It has been an unexpected gift to be home and write during this time. I've completed three other books and this poetry is my fourth.

As Shakti rewires me, my body, mind, and spirit recalibrate again and again, moving in and out of life's polarities. It is from these experiences of love, devastating loss and renewal, that I can lay before you the rawness of my heart and soul. This poetry is my offering of the full spectrum of love.

I have placed the poems in three realms, each reflecting a cycle of the soul, and layer of healing. These realms are:

The Underworld—where descent carves its path through grief and loss, where hidden wounds speak, and where the soul learns to sit in the dark until its eyes adjust to new sight.

The Mystery—where silence becomes fertile, and what cannot be named begins to move within. Here, prayers weave with uncertainty, and the unseen world offers its whispers of guidance and wonder.

Remembering - Rebirth - Renewal—where what once felt shattered or mysterious gives way to new life. From the ashes of sorrow and confusion, beauty, creativity, and love arise. This is not a return to what was, but a remembering of my pure essence. It is the blossoming of deeper truths, rooted in both the shadow of the underworld and the radiance of light where soul guides you.

My creative illness was an intense time of psychological upheaval and growth. The creative flow connected my rational, conscious mind with the deeper, symbolic world of the unconscious.

The dream world revealed the process—filled with grace—from the fire's ashes rose the ancient temple, The *Prima Materia* revealed the raw material of my psyche: the alchemical concept of a primordial substance. This was the cauldron of my mystical poetry.

Each image within the book is an etching of my original art and altars. They bridge the visual and poetic elements, and carry the archetypal and alchemical energies of the poetry.

As the surface layers of my art and altars were removed, something deeper was revealed—as if I had exposed their souls, naked and standing as altars unto themselves. What emerged feels sacred, as though the soul of the book breathed itself into form through these images, reflecting the unseen. Each image carries the soul of the poetry.

May this offering ignite your soul's fire.

Kerani Marie

The Underworld

Where descent carves its path through grief and loss, where hidden wounds speak, and where the soul learns to sit in the dark until its eyes adjust to new sight.

The Soul Realm
of the
Underworld

The Fury of Grief

My heart is tight
in the darkness
of shock and betrayal.
Dismay, hurt, and sadness
drip from my cells.
Stunned and wounded,
tears wait to burst free
from behind
the thin veil of living,
while dying inside.

I witness my journey
unraveling the tapestry of self.
Threads woven from the past,
through the present, and into the future
lose their grip.

The sharp sword of clarity
cuts through my illusion,
revealing the nakedness of my truth
standing in front of me.

The myth of the martyr is not love,
betraying myself ceases now.
Unconditional love returns to me.
The line is drawn in the sand.

Our holy union has completed its journey,
giving us our lessons and gifts
waving us on into our own holy union.

The heartache and struggle
were the needed push to let go.
The soul's path was the journey.
In love we began,
in love we set each other free.
2 - 19

Claws

How can I tell you,
my gut is wrenching,
my heart bleeds,
and my fury held at bay
waiting for the strategic moment
to lunge
and claw
the eyes out
of the dark and distorted one?

Fierce grief and
wrathful indignation
boil under my skin
while the truth is
waiting to be seen.
11 - 18

Pissed

I am royally enraged
the anger is fierce deep and primal
guttural sounds coming from my body
the roar of outrage.
I am pissed!
What the fuck!
Living alone sucks,
not having a partner sucks,
taking care of all this financial shit
is stressful and draining.

How is it he is on a vacation
and I am doing all this fucking stuff?
I want this to be done
so I can move on.
I fill stuck.
I feel enslaved
until it is done.
I feel pinned down
and jailed.
7 - 19

Clinched Fist

What lies inside
these clinched fists
the hurt
the anger
the fear
distain?

What lies behind being accused of not being
grateful and only wanting money?

What are his muddy feelings
and resistance to giving me money?

What brings out the look of distain and
dismissiveness?

How do you shift from considerate, kind and
gentle, to harsh cold detached and absolute?

How do you wear your mask and live
with yourself?

Sadness and discord permeate
this broken and scarred man.

It's wrong!
If he would just fix it
I wouldn't have to feel
these terrible feelings of:
Betrayal.
Disregard.
Unkindness.
Abandonment.
Fear.
Uncertainty.
Not being enough.

Feeling alone
not in partnership with life:
Disowned.
Punished.
Angry.
Rageful.
Disgusted.

Being angry and hurt with him
I don't have to deal with
my own anger at myself.

I heard a voice say.
'I know you heard
the sound in the night
and wondered what it was.
You know it was you screaming
Love yourself!'
4 - 19

Aching

Each cell wants to connect:
understand, process and discover.
Held back by fatigue, futility and dissolution
dying inside from what isn't my nature.
The call is strong, the will is greater.
The feeling is stunned despair,
sadness and disbelief.
I need help!
Aching to engage old ways.
Praying for the new ones
to take the lead,
I cry for help.
11 - 18

Unraveling

Heavy and frail
filled with sorrow and disbelief
hungry for it not to be so
grasping for the lost thread
to stop the unraveling.
There is no peace,
no place to land,
only unraveling,
the constant unraveling
of my life.
A tapestry of unraveling.
11 - 18

Excuses

Over and over again
I believed the excuses:
I'm tired.
I'm scared.
I'm confused.
I feel defended.
I feel controlled.
I feel guilty.
I don't speak what I feel well.
I forget.
I can't remember.
I might have.
I'm not sure.
I don't know what I feel.
I can't find the words.
I'm slow.
It takes me time.

It's a given – Even if I don't say it.
I'm not good at that.

EVEN IF ALL OF THIS WAS TRUE
IT STILL DOESN'T WORK
in an intimate, soulful relationship.
11 - 18

The One Who Hides

I feel you hiding, little one
Behind my eyes and in my cells
I feel how ashamed you are to be out
You hear your words, "I'm an imposter!"
Afraid they will find out
You're not who they think you are.

With tears in my eyes, I sob for your futility
trying to be what you're supposed to be,
I'm so, so sorry.
Tell me more about yourself
you don't need to hide anymore.

Through tears flowing and
the howls of pain, I hear:
"My head hurts, My head hurts
Oh God, it hurts so bad.
I'm not bad.
My jaw hurts.
I want to crawl into bed.
My throat hurts.

My jaw is shaking!”
I ask, “How can I help you?”
After a long silence
I assure her I can wait for a response,
"I’m here and value you."

Suddenly, I’m walking down the church aisle:
Oh my God! I’m in the Pink Wedding Dress.
I feel the shame and terror.
Wanting to run and hide,
The imposter— afraid of being seen as I am
the good and bad girl at odds.

I tell her, “I’m here to walk with you.”

Her scream echoes,
“I’m not bad, I’m not bad!”

I respond, "I’m walking with you."

She cries out, "My throat hurts. My throat hurts.”

Oh my gosh, I’m shaking again.
I notice I’m rubbing my skin in circles
Soothing myself, I reach out and say,
“I’m holding you – I’m holding you
I’m so sorry!
6 - 25

Not Enough

The agonizing reminder of
not being enough has come to visit.
Panic and fear are palpable.
The trembling limbs and core shaking
rattling my cage of adapting and spiritual bypass.
The not enough has been my nemesis
my fear, my dread.
Not enough money.
Not enough love.
Not enough time.
I know, I will die
if I don't have enough.
All is threatened:
I will suffer and
be annihilated.

Out of pure fear and aversion,
I choose differently.
Today, I make a friend
with my "not enough energy."
I listen to the message it shares,

I hear the wisdom it bestows,
I feel the deep roots as it tells me
I am strong like a redwood tree.
Enough is inside of me not out there.

I am held by the tree
taken to the place
where I am free,
alive and dancing with spirit
ready to feel,
ready to listen.

I promise
I will listen,
not run away again.
I will pay attention
knowing to turn inward.
Being Enough is inside,
not out there.

I fall and shake again,
this time I hear wisdom speak:

your umbilical cord was cut to soon
your life blood — oxygen taken too soon,
then there was no breath.
Mom said there wasn't enough,
not enough milk
for her to breastfeed.

A sigh of agony,
as truth permeates me.
I feel the fear.
I feel the loss.
I feel the lack of nourishment.
The root of Not Enough
is unearthed on
Earth Day.

Now, I know.
I understand.
I listened.
It is enough.
I am enough.
3 - 24

Fully Human

From the depths of the cauldron
lives the darkness of rage.
The luminous mist of love
and the cry of, "How could you?"
The heart's betrayal,
the body's anguish
and the endless compassion boil.
The echo of the thundering truth
lays the pearls at your feet.
Your broken heart
and vast love
are the medicine.
Now you are fully human.
10 - 18

Despair

Trust and intimacy falling away
despair comes in their place.
Fear and sadness dance around the discord,
unsettled confusion and betrayals stench,
swirling in the cauldron
gasping for an answer.
Clarity and direction are still miles away
sitting in this incessant fire.
An unwanted initiation,
a disregard and disappointment.

The dissolution and uncertainty
hovering over my belly like vultures
waiting, waiting for the final surrender.
The smell of burning flesh,
the flowing river of blood,
calling to be eaten =
All becomes the nectar.
11 - 18

Resilient

How? What? Why?
In disbelief, I rally
to overcome the pain
and to love again.

One more attempt
to understand
to look within.

One more time
to deepen the love and compassion,
forgiveness and resilience.

Let's try this.
Let's try that.

I am hurt and angry.

How could you say that?
How could you not understand?

Why! Why! Why!

Rage drifts in and out.
Love wins and I am back again.

Forgiveness.
Compassion.
Understanding.
Resilience.
For what end?
11 - 18

Sadness

The roots of sadness raise their shoots
into the light of day.
Unpredictable and copious they rise
leaving friends and family
arriving at my empty house.
The loss and disbelief grow weeds.
Sadness infuses my taste buds
and the bitter taste chokes me.
Why wasn't love's embrace enough?
11 - 18

Naked Grief

A rootless itinerant
I wander
in uncharted territory.
Unraveling and reorienting
Grief, the wild ride:
potent and rich
harsh and cutting
fertile and barren
drenched in tears,
I'm tumbled
colliding between
anger, then grace,
blessings, then profanity.

I descend into the abyss.
The bedrock trembles in darkness,
echoing the quaking
of my shattered heart.
Melting and freezing,
confused and trusting,
still in shell shock,
I soar into the unknown
being wise, then unreasonable,
humbled, then self-absorbed,
generous, then fearful.
Judging, then understanding.
I am everything and nothing,
I am naked grief
12 - 18

Howling

A roar of agony
bursts forth.
No warning.
A sound, a word, a thought
and the energies erupt
volcanic quaking.
This can't be real.
This sucks.
Why?
Fuckin why?
11 - 18

Looking

Why am I looking to him to feel safe,
comforted and intimate?
A place where I can find congruency
common ground, feelings,
purpose, and direction:
shared joy
a place to land and rest
arms of love,
trust, kindness, generosity.
What happened?
Where is it?
Why did it go?
Was it there or was it my projection?

I am angry and stunned,
confused, shocked
and bewildered –
baffled, perplexed.
In dismay and alarming confusion
I search for something that is not there.
It's not in him, but in me.

It feels unnatural
to not have a shared reality
and emotional journey.
Someone is supposed to be there
to listen and hold my tender heart
and to have empathy and give support:
a shared reality.
1 - 19

Dismembered

Through all the muck
the swamp of mire
and thick mud
the barbed wire of
resistance and obstacles
to my destination.

I must move toward my soul.
I look back and see what
I love.
I want what I loved.
I want my family close.
I want to give and share love.
I want connection and intimacy.
I can have some of this
if I compromise my soul.

Can I accept the painful void of soul and depth?
I look ahead and there is the light of freedom.
Yet, the mud and mire keep me entangled,
resisting my every move.

Moving forward is exhausting.
I am so angry and sad.
I am furious that I have to move again.
Sell my home;
figure out where I will live.
pack and unpack again and again.
It is getting so old and I am old and tired.
It really sucks.

How do I navigate the dismemberment,
the chaos,
feeling ungrounded,
the unraveling of myself?
Who Am I in all this?
All my identities swirling
nothing is settling.

Initiated in the fire,
Dismembered,
I am raw and tender.
Please help me!
1 - 19

Say Something

Please say something so I can feel better.
Please tell me you're hurting too.
Tell me this is hard.
Tell me you regret how this all happened.
Tell me how much you appreciated
what we had and things changed in you,
and it had nothing to do with me.

Don't tell me how happy you are and
how this works for you.
How can you be so detached?
How can you disconnect so easily?
How is this possible?
It is excruciatingly painful!

Tell me something!
My pain is more than I can bear.
Say something so I can feel better.
1 - 19

The Mystery

Where silence becomes fertile, and what cannot be named begins to move within. Here, prayers weave with uncertainty, and the unseen world offers its whispers of guidance and wonder.

THE SOUL REALM
OF THE
MYSTERY

Now What

What happens when I'm finished,
when my four new books are published:
the sequel to *Emerging Woman*,
the story of my two Shakti Kundalini Passages,
my Mystical Artistry Journey,
my *Naked at the Altar* poetry book.
Then, what?

I created three spiritual centers,
been on three vision quests,
and three spiritual pilgrimages,
built an Underworld Womb Cave,
been married three times,
birthed two children,
have four grandchildren and,
seven great grandchildren,
traveled the world.
Now, what?

I feel spiritually rich.
My emotional intelligence is strong.
My gratitude is vital.
I create art and poetry.
I'm an elder and wisdom keeper.
Now, what?

This has been a theme in my life,
always knowing there is more
More what?
Now, What?

Polarities play with me.
I'm living with a
dense heavy dull energy within me.
It pervades my energy field.
What is it?
Is it mine or my ancestors?
Is it mine or the collective?
Regardless, I feel it.

I am swimming
in an ocean of love.
Everything is love.
My senses are magnified.
What I see or feel is pure love
I am in a rarified field of creation.

I know . . . put in proper spacing.
It is the next unknown moment
overflowing in possibilities.
9 - 25

Loss

No matter what your belief is of the afterlife,
no matter how you hold the big picture,
either your loved one
is in heaven
out of pain now,
or merged with the all,
with the universal spirit,
or will reincarnate or
become a spiritual guide.

There is loss.
There is separation.
There is sorrow.
There is grief.
There is shock.
There is anger and longing.
12 - 24

A Sacred Relationship

Can Ego rule,
and Soul follow?
Can Soul lead,
and Ego follow?
What happens when they dance
no longer split,
living in the heart
as a Sacred Relationship?
6 – 25

Presence of the Unknown

I awoke dis-jointed, bewildered,
swimming in helpless rage.
The collective loss, the crisis swirling
navigating polarities,
tragedies and spiritual bypass
dancing in my body.

Do I live where I create my reality,
ignoring parallel universes?
Do I fight,
do I pray,
do I run,
do I isolate?

I feel the deep old rage
creeping out of the shadows.
Helplessness, at the core of my being,
held hostage by others' control and values.

My external life of parents and teachers,
supervisors and governments

told me how to be, act, feel,
to be quiet, sit still and listen,
Do as you are told!
They taught me how to be a woman,
a wife, a mother, a professional,
my soul screamed for more.

I'm still wearing shame like a warm coat
woven as I walked down the isle
in a pink wedding dress.
Pregnant, and no longer a virgin.

Then, the Sun whispered:
You don't need this anymore.

I watch birds fly free,
the sun illuminating mountain tops,
a cardinal perched on the courtyard table,
music vibrating my cells,
the wind carrying whispers of possibility.

I live it all!

Divinely blessed to be alive,
feeling quakes in my bones,
a quiver in my jaw,
the scream building in my solar plexus.
I hear the roaring voices within:
Live in the present.
Create your own reality.
Put energy into what serves life.
Don't bypass what you feel.
Be kind to yourself.
Stay informed.
Be aware.
Stand in your truth.

You are not alone.
Live in the presence
Trust the unknown.
Listen to your dreams.
Love more.
Breathe.
4 - 25

Flashpoint

Is there a flashpoint
where Evil and Divinity meet?
Where the sacred empathy of compassion
and the brutality of narcissistic abuse
touch and bleed into each other
creating something new?

The goodness and sacred intimacy
of humans
alongside the evil and cruel
actions toward each other
is all happening,
all real,
all felt and seen.

In my naivety,
I felt that once the evil energies
meet the energies of goodness,
the evil energies would want to change.
Once the truth of love was heard
there would be no more evil.

In my elder years,
I see this has not happened.

Do we stand in the middle
hold hands with both,
weave a new tapestry,
dance between the worlds
And acknowledge that
both evil and goodness
lives in all of us
What we choose to do
is our freedom.
6 - 25

The Long Arc of Integration

They never tell you how long it takes –
not because it should be rushed,
but because it can't be.
Kundalini does not arrive
as a gentle whisper.
She roars through the body
like a wildfire,
illuminating everything you've hidden,
everything you've clung to,
everything you thought was you.
In the wake of her rising,
the body trembles,
the mind unravels,
the soul remembers.
and then begins the slow work–
not of "healing,"
but of becoming spacious enough
to hold the truth she left behind.

It is a shedding,
a recalibrating,
a dying and birthing,
often many times over.
The nervous system must rewire.
The heart must grieve.
The spirit must learn how to wear a body again.
This is not a crisis.
This is an initiation.
There is no map.
Only listening.
Only surrender.
Only trust in the wisdom
that what takes time to integrate
was never meant to be rushed.
Some wounds are not wounds at all—
just unopened gateways.
And some healing is not healing,
but remembering who you've always been.
8 - 25

Fiercely Alive

Kundalini doesn't obey methods or mantras—
it dismantles them.
It burns through the layers,
takes you where you didn't plan to go.
It's a wild ride—
raw, holy, and fiercely alive.
8 - 25

Shakti Kundalini's Way

She roared
alive in my dreams
explosive fire and destruction—
the old temple burned,
the ancient stone altar remained
not destroyed, but exposed.

My dreams mirror
the awakened and
shattered ego.
The outer temple consumed,
the eternal presence left.
Fire is not an ending—
ruins are the beginning

of a deeper foundation
upon which
the golden threads
of my journey
can be woven.
6 - 25

The Womb's Seduction

The womb is the cauldron,
the vessel of fire
and mystery.

Its seduction
is not a lure of flesh
but the primal pull
of the soul
toward the undoing of the ego.

To be seduced
by the womb
is to be summoned
into the dark heat
where life and death mingle,
where all certainties
melt into possibility.
5 - 25

Abundant Grace and Sacred Rage

How did I slip from grace
and a sacred focus
on qualities that serve life,
on ways to transmute negativity into gold,
on sending love and light to all beings
walking in gratitude and bliss?

Was it the short Ted talk
of a courageous woman fighting for her life
from the insidious tech companies
having access to everything about her,
using information as a witch hunt against her?
Seeing the lies and revenge alive in the world
attacking and controlling others is not ok.
Now, I am enraged, shaking and ready to fight.

As I struggle wondering
can I just live in grace all the time,
I feel the anger and disgust
over what is happening
in the world,

in my country,
between people.
No, I need to fight like hell
for human decency and rights.
Standing right in the middle
of the two polarities,
I realize I can't fix it.
They are both alive and valid parts
of my lived experience.

I live with, and in all of this.
Do I just be and live in the in-between
waiting for something new to emerge?
Can I stand in the wholeness of love and life
with ferocious truth
and contagious compassion?
Can I be patient and diligent
knowing the insights will come
out of the stillness between
abundant grace and sacred rage?
6 - 25

My 80th Year

I wonder
is this it?
Is this what I have lived for:
To stand at the center
where the paradoxes and polarities meet,
feeling a rush of comfort, delight, and fulfillment,
a sense of AWE
satiated with life's wonders and losses,
with my time on earth
coming closer
to its expiration date . . .
Can this be it?

I have spent my life
yearning and striving for
enlightenment and
awakened realization.
To find this
I dance with it all,
a place of ease and dynamic tension
in-between the polarities

where something new can emerge.
This Soulful relationship
supersedes spiritual bypass
and ego’s struggle
leaving me
face to face with all that is.

It is a mobius strip,
an infinity symbol of constant movement
colored with diverse paradoxical experiences:
The shriek of delight as my eyes behold
the light upon the mountain.
Roars of grief's agony when
I lose my loved ones.
The rape and pillage of Mother Earth,
to the divine music and dance of creation.
The delicate flowers' beauty and birds’ song,
humanity's abuses to each other.
The river's refreshing scent and mist
the starvation and wars.
The innocent smiles of the little ones,
and twinkle in the lover's eyes.

Fifty years after reading about the paradox
where everything matters and nothing matters,
where you can be in the world, but not of it.
Where all beings are perfection perfecting
on the sacred journey of being human,
life is as it is.
Not as we want it.
Yet, it is what remains as we see it and feel it.
Nothing is wrong
only the dance of life's mystery.
I celebrate it all—This is it
brewing in the caldron of
My eightieth year.
2 - 25

Cauldron of life

Life's journey
is alive with intense
polarities and paradoxes:
Changes in our solar system.
Political extremes.
Worldwide rebellions .
Extreme weather patterns.
Divisive radicalization.
Beautiful art and music.
Humanitarian efforts.
Deep generosity.
Kindness and sacrifice.
Creative genius.

My vision becomes blurred
with tears of joy, wonder and sadness.

As all of this swirls within me I can be with change,
I can open to something and new and curious as to
how this will unfold.

I want to be engaged,
participative and be active around it.
With a flick of a switch
I'm disconnected from it,
only experiencing my life,
nature's beauty and grace
smelling the whiff of
my self-centered nature.
A sense of denying the distress
and futility for the world
creeps in
even though I know
I can only change my inner world.

Catapulted, I'm in the realm of
everything matters and nothing matters.
I'm feeling the double bind–
A familiar energy occupies me.
An identity filled with
struggle and helplessness,
a mandate and victim lives here.

I must make a choice or do something.
What do I choose to create
in this moment of being alive?
Deep gratitude creeps in
for a life so free and rich.

I wonder:
How is it I have this life?
How am I
not in Gaza, Ukraine or Africa?
The suffering of other human beings
lives in me.
I pray for them.
I hurt for them.
I am grateful, disillusioned and angry.

All of the
freedom-fear-love-projections-ideals
live within my parameters
Anger-rage-sadness rise and
I want to run away—enough, enough!

Blessed-grace-filled-humble-flowing-
unraveling-emerging-magic-
all eclipse my heart.

A love affair with intimacy
with what is - as it is
disgust–fear-uncertain
futility-confusion-disorientation and
gratitude are alive.

All is - as it is
in the cauldron of life.
3 - 25

Excavating Ancestral Territory

Fierce energies of sadness and rage
surface as a volcanic eruption.
I feel the need to blame.
I want the other gone.
Feeling the pattern of
my raw human reaction,
I must rid myself of the outside cause.

Abruptly, I stop
at the center of my whirlwind.
I feel the energy swirling.
I embodied these feelings.
They are mine.
I want to know more,
to find the gold of their wisdom.

The clarity of this distress
reveals its cycle of existence
in the ancestral family linage.
It is time to change the trajectory,

time to create something different.
I spoke out to the one I blamed.
I reported the distress of anger and sadness
for all the years this has been perpetuated.

Then, more gold was excavated
during my healing session,
I was this ancestral energy.

Then, coming out of myself
another me emerged standing strong
in the power of the divine feminine warrioress.
I morphed back and forth
between these identities.

I felt a tower of power and protection
lodged in my shoulder.

Not stuck energy,
instead, a well-placed
system of protection
guarding me from the

intrusions and uninvited energies
of other's desires and demands,
cultural dictates
and false identity.
I, again felt my mother
using this same arm and shoulder
to protect herself from her father's violence.
I felt the patriarchal ancestral energies
suffocating the feminine.

As I acknowledged its existence
the pillar softened.
Now, there was room for gentleness.
Then, a stake in my neck surfaced—
it held the counter tension to my shoulder.
Energetically removing it,
I feel a sense of loss
as well as being lost,
as the reorganizing occurred.
What remained was
gratitude and love.
5 - 25

Self-Love - The New Empathy

The woven shroud of empathy
cloaks true intimacy.
The threads of love,
kindness and compassion
override one's own needs.

Love is showered upon others,
our heart enriched and full
satisfied and abundant now.

Yet, the continued cloaking
generates a numbness—
My need for intimacy is ignored.
My identity rising
as kindness and understanding,

Until one day
the cloak falls away
and the starkness
of what was sacrificed remains:

My own gratification of giving,
took the place of true intimacy.

Stunned,
I turn inward.
No better day or time
for Self-Love - the New Empathy.
1-19

Until the NO Comes

All is good, workable
filled with possibilities
until the NO comes.

What seemed supple and permeable
turns into a sharp jagged NO,
shattering my sensibilities.

The NO
to empathy and intimacy,
respect and consideration,
shocks me.

Then, I realize
empathy only lived in me
and my world shatters.

NO becomes the catapult
throwing me out of my illusion
to the other side.

Here, I find my NO,
my boundaries
my soul.

NO!

To empathy replacing Intimacy.
No, to ignoring my needs.
No, to what isn't soulful.
No, to excuses.

Yes, to self-love.
Yes, to self-compassion.
Yes, to boundaries.
Yes, to my soulful truth.

Before NO,
there was illusion.
1-19

The In-Between

What lies between this no-place and emptiness,
between abundance and loss, love and grief,
this place, where no one wants to go?

The tension between the polarities
a field where neither live
and both are present,
This place where movement stops
where nothing is clear
confusion and doubt prevail,
life feels futile and heavy.

Then, my head pops up
through the veil of polarities.
I can breathe again.
Like the turtle breaks through
the water's shelf and gathers air,
I come up for air, then dive again
over and over.
When will I rest in the abundance
and love again?

When will the grief and loss
become a gentle memory?
When will I love myself fully?
1-19

We Choose

As I stepped into the grocery line
the closed sign went up.
as I moved to the next register.
A man steps into the closed line
gently I say, “It’s closed.”
He hesitates and says,
“Thanks for policing me.”

Surprised, I felt discord inside.
He didn’t accept my help.
Instead, I was his enemy.
He moves behind me.
I feel threatened by
someone seeing life from his angle,
I breathe and find my center.

Seeing he has only a few things
I offer to let him go ahead of me.
He kindly says, "No, thank you!
Continuing, he apologizes.
"You are a kind person,
I overacted, I don't like being told what to do,
I didn't see the closed sign
until you pointed it out.
I'm sorry. I feel so foolish."

I smiled, considering my words,
feeling and seeing my thoughts of
"We are our own worst enemy,"
as I bathe in the alchemy of
two people's reactions
becoming kindness.
3 - 25

Cosmic Soup

My senses collide
raw, vital, and potent.

An emotional eruption
A kaleidoscope of experience.
I’m enlivened on this human journey.

All is revealed vying for my attention:
A primal longing,
a sense for what is real.
The cosmic soup
churning in my womb.
My inner cauldron fueled by the fire,
a pure and essential desire.

Deep sorrow, Rage,
Exquisite love, Gratitude,
Expansive and Contractive Waves
of life's journey shaking me.
I hear howling growls,
whimpers of innocent outrage
urging me in and out of perplexity.

Re-sculpting my foundation,
my ravenous hunger
furiously grasping,
deeply unsatisfied
crying out to be soothed,
"Feed me, feed me!"
My soul is calling.
8 - 24

Remembering

Where what once felt shattered
or mysterious gives way to new life.
This is not a return to what was, but a
remembering of my pure essence. It is the
blossoming of deeper truths, rooted in both the
shadow of the underworld and the radiance
of light where soul guides you.

The Soul Realm
of
Remembering

Sea of Love

A wave of energy comes through me.

I was swimming in a sea of love,
everything was love:
The ring on my finger.
The sound of the bird.
My phone.
The mountains in the distance.

Anything and everything my eyes saw,
my body felt, were all love.

I was in a field of Love.
I was it and it was profound.

The gratitude and the freedom
was extraordinary and
I feel blessed.
9 - 25

The Other Place

I find myself
in an odd
but familiar space.
A different reality
displaced my stability,
joy and delight.

It showed up shuddering,
a jerky movement of my body,
then, an ache in my back and neck.
While confusion seeped into my life
and my legs began to stumble,
I wondered,
where did the ease and lightness go?

Now, I am heavy, dense
wanting to curl up in a fetal position,
cry, yell and feel my anger rise.
Before, I was singing,
excited about life,
in so much gratitude.

Now, it is dark in here
as I look for my gratitude.
I am as surprised about it coming
as I will be about it going.
11 - 25

No Concepts

What if each experience was just that—
a direct and complete experience
through the senses.

No need to categorize
or conceptualize
how and why,
no explanation or need to understand
just the raw primal and wild moment.
4 - 24

Layers of Revelation

I see the mysterious
weaving of my life.
Beyond the ancestral culture.
Beyond the societal norms.
Beyond my own desires.

More is at play.
There is sculpting and
weaving from the unseen,
where soul and the mystery
dance to their delight —
while my ego flails in the
discord, anger, pain and disgust
swirling within me.

I'm shown
how each moment
was an orchestrated unfolding.

Each crisis necessary
in the unraveling and rearranging
of the characters in my life,
so they can move
into their soul's dance
while I did mine.
11 - 25

Grace and Love

The accolades reach my heart
The tender words feel soothing
when exaggerated they don't resonate.

A disconnect is exposed
their motive is questioned.

My ego is activated.

When their soul speaks,
it is nectar, nourishing and alive.

When their ego speaks,
the words fall to the ground
heavy and dense.

In-between is a place for grace
like the struggle of what was
and what is coming
is a place of grace and love.
7 - 25

Grace Visits

The fog has lifted
the layers of discord gone.
I'm here naked
imbued with
the grace of love
the potency of gratitude
and the delight of wonder.
11 - 25

Crack in Reality

The fabric of creation
has cracked.
I see through it.

With each encounter
more layers of ego's illusion
drop away.

More energy fields of identity
are revealed.

Each unique reality interacting
within the whole,
each with their own sense of what is real
committed to its way of life.

I am the observer
while I dance between the worlds.
consciousness lives
emerging from the Quantum Field:

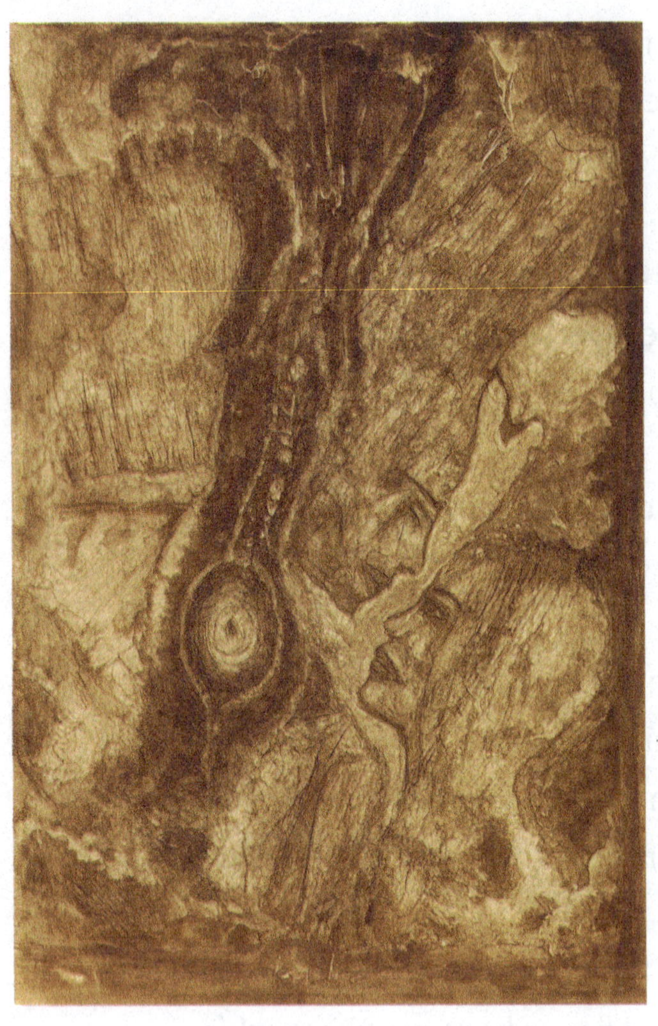

Living within a cell,
a sperm, an egg,
from cells uniting,
dividing and duplicating,
creating something new.

From an embryo to an infant
Each fully immersed in its moment
It's unique expression.

In time the toddler,
child and teenager surface,
each is consumed with its own reality
of experiences and perceptions.

Each moment,
each layer of reality
playing out the parts of life.
Each person finding their way and
learning to discover more interplay
and interactions predicated on how
each experience was integrated.

How conscious choice was enlivened
fueled by the unconscious and their soul's journey.

From the vantage point of the crack
I see adult children attempting to fulfill their
desire of wanting to connect with the other,
trying to satisfy the ego and feeling the soul's call
consumed by a limited reality.
There is a spiraling and repetition,
the constant and unconscious quest
for a common ground
to stand in their wholeness,
to know their original self,
the unified truth,
Quantum reality.

The layers of identity are distinct
dense and difficult to transcend.
Where is the equal playing ground between,
the cell and the lumberjack,
the child and the race driver,
the pacifist and the aggressor,

the artist and engineer?
The layers of consciousness
with the baseline of ego and
the potential of the soulfulness,

all moving within the interplay of
its perfect imperfection:
No good or bad,
and divine timing.
Wisdom reveals itself
as we crawl, walk, and run along
the evolutionary journey,
discovering it is all
nature's playground.

From the ego's narcissism
to individuation and evolution
where a sense of other and we emerge,
and soulfulness is vital and alive,
we hear the echo of illumination.
We are home.
5 - 25

Supernova

An explosion
shatters my matter
and what matters.

Marking the end
of my life
as it was

I am pierced
by the intense light
of grace and love.

I am a supernova
1 - 19

Weave the Sacred

Kundalini is the serpent
who travels all worlds
descending into the Underworld
to burn away illusion,
rising to the Upperworld
to reveal divine light,
and flowing through the Middle World
to weave the sacred
into the fabric of everyday life.

Healing is not
only about soothing
the wound,
but listening to its message.
In its fire
lies an invitation
to restore flow,
to claim safety,
and to honor
the boundaries
protecting the tender heart.
9 - 25

Initiated in the Cauldron of Life

Dismembered and stripped raw
in the Cauldron of Life,
I'm humbled and blessed
with eyes wide open,
wisdom my companion,
I step through the threshold
in awe and wonder
the mystery is revealed.
I AM FREE
11 - 24

The Process

Stability
is not the absence
of challenge—
It is the capacity
to stay present
with what arises.
You are still progressing.
You are still being
held by this process,
even in the unraveling
8 - 25

The Divine Human

The Alchemy of Kundalini
is the deep transformation
of the human
into the divine human.
It dismantles,
purifies,
and rewires me
so my body
becomes a temple,
my mind becomes a mirror,
and my life
becomes an offering.
8 - 25

Womb of Transformation

All initiation
is a passage
through the underworld,
a descent
into the womb
of transformation
where one's essence
is remade.
8 - 25

The Bestower of Love

I kissed:
The sheets protecting my plants from frost.
The cup holding my morning tea.
A song enlivening my love and gratitude.
The glorious delight of being alive.
My body infused with tender moments.

My eyes kissed beauty:
Gratitude danced
across the landscape of my life.
My hand touched my lips
awaiting a kiss.

I wondered why these things
want to be kissed.
Why I want to kiss them.
Washed over by shear truth,
I can see - I make life sacred.

I infuse and bathe things in love.
Everything becomes inseparable.
Awaiting my kiss
I am the repository
the bestower of love.
9 - 25

Medicine Wheel

There is a sacred hoop,
a medicine wheel
holding us in all directions
as we navigate life.
The powers of this circle are
love, forgiveness,
unity of all elements,
plant medicines, animal spirits,
Mother Earth and Father Sky.

They do not worry
about whether you have made
wise choices or poor ones.
They are far too rooted
in the ever-changing present moment.
Working together, they weave
a blanket just for you.
It will protect you
and keep you warm
as you walk your path
wherever it may lead.
7 - 25

Fruits of Love

I'm sending love to your heart
to the souls who are suffering
or who lost their lives,
to the perpetrators
who have lost their souls.

Each person receives this love
through the filters of their lived experience.
I know the seed of love is planted
and depending on the terrain,
the divine timing of new life will
flourish into abundant
fruits of love
6 - 25

Sacred Well

The Kundalini, like a sacred well,
does not pour endlessly.

It rises when the vessel is ready
and recedes,
when the soul must sit in stillness.

Both the flood
and the drought
serve the becoming.
8 - 25

Being

I am in the Soul's
world now
in the vast,
uncharted territory
of the unconscious.

The spirit world
where time dissolves,
agendas fade,
and being itself
becomes the only compass.
9 - 25

No Magic Bullet

No pill.
No wand.
No fix to soothe or stop the storm.
7 - 25

Myself

The fire is out,
The ground still smolders.
I am no longer who I was—
And yet, I am more deeply myself.
9 - 25

Borneo's Magic

The river is our gateway:
Alive and wild.
Cells imprinted with newness.
Molecules dance differently.
The forest re-sculpts us.
Surprise encounters.
Proboscis monkeys play in the trees.
Orangutang gather for bananas.
Birds reveal their colorful loftiness.
Rain cleanses the city's grit/
I am here!

Colorful and tasty food delight.
Black and brown rivers meet.
A deep mysterious portal is revealed.
Lightning bugs play with our senses.
The sounds awaken our primal and wild nature.
The hierarchy is displayed,
and we are transformed.
Lightning jolts us
into the moment of fear and trust.

The quantum field
permeates life anew.
Now, I swing with the orangutang.
I squeal with the hornbill bird.
I rattle the roof with my playfulness.
I am still and present as the green snake.
10 - 24

Soar with the Mystery

May we embody this human spiritual life
dancing between the worlds,
connecting our hearts and souls.
Walking through life
with the golden cord
nurtured by the Primal Mother's milk,
Supported by the Great Father Spirit,
held in the arms of all that is.
Discovering life's beauty and wonder
may our spirits soar with the Mystery.
8 - 25

Unconditional Love

My unconditional love felt boundless.
Yet, through the rubble of dismay and shock
the potency of deeper love and grace
REMAINED alive.
My flesh and blood infused with love
becoming my solace and hope
mirroring the richness of my heart.
Love is a vibrational field
surrounding and permeating others,
yet, only as much as can be taken in,
only what can be integrated,
loves transformative power awaits
their invitation.
It is a choice to feel its potency, to receive
its vital force and transformative experience.
Love doesn't change a soul's journey,
the choice is theirs.
Their life, covenants and commitments
are only as deep as the people who make them.
Unconditional Love can't change that.
11 - 18

Live your Truth

Give up being right.
Be true to yourself.
That's enough.

Beliefs do not go hand and hand
with proving you are right.
The freedom is living your truth.

When you let go
of your ego's need to be right
of thinking you know what's best for others,
true freedom will be your ground.
An energy that creates an ease
the field of connection with others
becomes enhanced.

I do take a stand
when your beliefs harm or limit
others' rights to be,
I speak out.

Lack of human rights are
a fight worth fighting against,
worth getting in good trouble for.

Give up being right!
Live your truth.
7 - 25

When My Family Roots Shifts

When my family roots begin
to fragment, rot, or drift away,
I feel the ground beneath me tilt—
a quiet, trembling shift.

When they entwine with other soil,
with circles not my own,
I'm left feeling loosened,
unmoored, undermined.

I want the sameness to remain—
the steady structure,
the who and how and what we were—
a constant pulse
in my heart,
my bones,
my roots.

Please come back,
I plead.
I know you.

I'm afraid for all of us
with you gone.

I'm guessing
when I left the family
root ball
to pursue my spiritual path,
they may have felt
this way about me.
10 - 25

The Dance

Existing in the opposites,
creating the wholeness,
confused and enlightened,
the pulse of life's rhythms
inform and shape us.

Through grace and grit,
to expansion and contraction,
feeling tight and infinite,
grasping and opening,
feeling oppression and freedom,
despair and potential
we saunter through dark and light.

Walking with opposites,
finding the gold,
the gems of wisdom,
the kernels of light and dark,

from the depths of agony and despair,
to joyous love and delight,
we dance through life.

Opposites so potent:
Filled with possibilities
waiting to be discovered.
Unearthed and exposed
the energies recycled
compost for a new creation.

The base elements
dancing through us
as we find
the gold of our spirit.
4 -19

Unearthing the Underworld Womb Cave

From before my birth,
the Great Mother Archetype
the Womb and the Wound,
were woven into
the fabric of my existence.

Culture minimized my innate
connection to the natural world,
disregarding my soulful being,
cutting my archetypal threads
from the roots of my primal mother.

Molded to fit in, I shrank and dried up.
Beauty and appearance came before the soul.
Guilt and shame overrode being wild and free.

Shrinking and acting the part
ate away at my life force,
conforming and wanting to be loved
overrode my innate knowing.

When my womb was impregnated at seventeen,
alcohol was the river of consciousness.
When my womb was slugged
by the baby's father
hoping it would start my period,
when an aunt created a concoction
hoping after I drank it, I would abort,
I felt small and betrayed.
Guilty and filled with shame,
confused, conflicted and lost.

My mother asked why I would have sex?
Demanding I had to marry in a pink dress,
Insisting I hold my stomach in
on my wedding day,
walking down the aisle the voice in my head
screaming, “I am not a bad girl!”

Sixty years after my son’s birth
and fifty-five years of spiritual
and emotional healing
cultivating a connection to the natural world,

exploring my divine feminine essence,
trusting my innate intuition and soulful life,
I was called to build an Underworld Womb Cave.
The Primal Mother and archetypal energies
were clear, potent and permeated my being.

Grace and visions flooded my world.
Inspiration, creativity and listening led my way.
The Divine Masculine showed up
creating the structure.
I remained open to what wanted to be born,
listening and feeling into how I would
open a portal into sacred space.

Humbled and filled with respect for this honor,
the grace-filled vision was manifest.
Seven months from inception to creation,
with the shared wisdom of seven birth doulas,
the Underworld Womb Cave was consecrated.

The week before the consecration
of the Womb Cave,

I began to sense karmic change entering the field.
This shift was clarified two days after
the Womb Cave's consecration,
when my children's father passed
from this worldly plane.

The complete circle of life and death
danced in my womb.

After many ceremonies and rituals in the
Underworld Womb Cave,
through the tears, prayers, gratitude, howls,
drumming, songs, surrendering and celebrations,
I was awakened into my own embodied truth.

The Womb Cave was built to heal my womb,
the wombs of all women and the hearts of men.

The Underworld Womb Cave
was to be honored and receive offerings
for her Soulful, Wild, Iconic Expression.

Alive within her creation portal,
the Primal Mother's Infinite Potential
offers herself as a spiritual friend.

The Underworld Womb Cave:
My offering for deeply healing
the feminine and masculine energies,
forward and back in time,
to remember who we are and
to stand in the wholeness of love,
embracing all aspects of being human.

Spirit, matter, and energy,
dancing and weaving life.

"I humbly stand in grace
Tempered by the fire
Of the womb cauldron
Bowing to the mystery of
The Underworld Womb Cave."
6 - 25

As I Am

When I want nothing from another
I get to see them for who they are
and I get to show up as I am.
10 - 25

In the Mystery, I became a living poem, offering my journey through words and grace. May these poems ignite the spark of new life waiting to emerge within you, just as it has for me. The Primal Mother has revealed — "Everything begins and ends in the Womb."

Kerani Marie
Sedona, Arizona, 2025

Kerani Marie

Kerani Marie is a Soulful Inner Wisdom Guide with over five decades of immersion in multicultural spiritual teachings and healing practices. Her wisdom is rooted in lived experience—through spiritual awakening, healing crises, and the alchemy of emerging into wholeness and freedom.

She is an artist, author, ceremonial teacher, and creative muse helping others to bring their stories and art to life. Kerani's authentic heart inspires the conscious emergence of souls through her writing, art, rituals, and retreats. She is also a Craniosacral Practitioner, Reiki Master, and founder of The Underworld Womb Temple, The Center for Living Wisdom, The Soulgazm Rendezvous, and Romancing Grief—Alchemy of Heartbreak.

Her books include *The Cycle of Life Journey, Emerging Woman: A Rite of Passage from Shame to Freedom, From the Tomb to Womb: The Alchemy of Love, Loss and Re-birth, Naked at the Altar of Soul: Poetry from the Soul Realms of the Underworld, Mystery and Renewal,* and soon to be published *Sacred Continuum: Soulful and Mysterious Encounters with Shakti Kundalini* and *Mystical Artistry: The Union of Art and Soul.*

Kerani lives in Sedona, Arizona, where she continues to guide others in embodying the sacred through love, grief, and creative awakening.

I would love to stay in
sacred connection with you.

Visit: www.KeraniMarie.com
Email: Kerani@KeraniMarie.com

Scan the QR code below
to connect with me on social media.

Gratitude

My heart is filled with abundant gratitude as I bathe in the realm of creative grace.

We have all heard that it takes a tribe to bring a book into the world. The truth of this lives in the hearts of those who supported my journey. My gratitude is overflowing. To Brenda Littleton, for her tireless, soulful, and insightful suggestions; to Lucid Design, Bill Georgevich, and Melanie Pahlmann for expertly carrying my manuscript through to its final stages—shaping it into book form, designing the cover, and making it available to the public.

To Pam Taylor, Enocha Ranjita Ryan, Milli Cannata, and Sharon Collaros for their generosity of time and reflection while reading Naked at the Altar and offering their creative insights.

And to my sister, Kathleen Hannum, for listening to each poem as it was birthed—thank you for being such a steady and loving presence.

Your Voice Matters: Leave a Review

If *Naked at the Altar of Soul* moved you, your words may help another woman find her own healing path.

Leaving a short, honest review is one of the most meaningful ways to support this work. It helps others discover the book and feel less alone in their own transformation.

You can leave your review on:

- The retailer's website where you purchased the book
- Goodreads — a space where readers share and discover books they love

Thank you for being part of this sacred journey.
Your voice matters.

OFFERINGS

Related Books and Audio from

SoWISE Creations

Where stories come to life!

SOFTCOVER

GRANDMOTHER SPIRIT SPEAKS SERIES:

BOOK 1

Emerging Woman:

A Rite of Passage from Shame to Freedom

BOOK 2

From the Tomb to Womb:

The Alchemy of Love, Loss and Re-birth

Cycle of Life Journey:

52 Journeys of Self-Awareness

with 12 experiential exercises

AUDIOBOOKS

Emerging Woman:
A Rite of Passage from Shame to Freedom

Cycle of Life Journey:
52 Journeys of Self-Awareness
with 12 experiential exercises
and bonus material: 52 radio interviews
exploring each Cycle of Life Journey

SoWISE Creations

offers a broad spectrum of author services including mentoring, book development, editing, publishing, audio recording, and web presence. Our mission is to assist woman (and men) who want to share the stories of their own soulful evolution.

For more information about bringing your book to life, please visit www.SoWISEcreations.com

Made in the USA
Coppell, TX
06 January 2026

68123331R00089